My Story
for
His Glory

The Goodness and Mercy of God
in the Midst of Life's Ups and Downs

Charity Dina

Nukan Publications

My Story for His Glory
*(The Goodness and Mercy of God in the Midst of
Life's Ups and Downs)*
By Charity Dina

Copyright © 2021 Charity Dina

ISBN: 979-8-848-12475-0

Publisher: Nukan Publications
Basildon, Essex, UK

First Printed in: 2023

Cover Design: Bailey Z. Landon

Copyright Notices

Dedication

I dedicate this book to God and the Father of our Lord Jesus Christ; for His Goodness and Mercy that have been demonstrated continuously in my life.

He has been my source of Strength, Songs and Inspiration.

I owe everything that I have, that I have, and will ever be to Him.

Papa God, You are awesome!

.

CONTENTS

Acknowledgments

I wish to acknowledge a number of people whom only eternity will reveal the immeasurable roles that they played in my life right from my conversion to Christ till date.

These worthy persons include:

Rev. Dr. Wilson Ezeofor, whose message was used by God to bring me to Christ.

Rev. Dr. Williams Okoye, whose teachings were used by God to give me foundational understanding of the Christian faith.

Rev. Samuel Shittu, whose teachings on prayers and his prayer life were used by God to infuse the passion for prayer and fasting into me.

Dr. Tunde Bakare who remains a model of truthfulness, integrity, consistency and a true father in the Ministry whose wisdom, knowledge of God and His Words have been a source of encouragement, direction, strength and inspiration to me.

.

Foreword

The book, "MY STORY FOR HIS GLORY" is my wife, Charity's first book and it gives me great pleasure to write its foreword.

Before you, is a work that tells about several life defining moments, experiences and events that turned out to be opportunities for the Lord to show forth His faithfulness, power and mercy and thereby brought glory to Himself.

From the very first chapter of "MY STORY FOR HIS GLORY" to the last chapter, you the reader, will be thrilled to read about how faith in God, prayers and obedience to God turned the tide, and victory was won to the glory of God.

That life is full of challenges is a given. However, what the outcome of the trials we face will turn out to be is dependent on our willingness to cooperate with

God and commit to having His will to be done and the glory to be His and His alone.

As you read this book with an open heart, your faith in God's ability to cause all things to work for the good of those who love Him and are called according to His purpose, will be further boosted.

You will be challenged to seek more of God through prayers and reading of His Word with the intent of obeying Him.

Charity, my wife of more than 34 years of marriage, is a proof that the story of our life can bring glory to God, as He demonstrates His Sovereignty, Mercy, Faithfulness and Goodness in all that life throws at us and as we commit to trusting Him even when we may not be able to trace Him.

May your own story, too, be for God's glory!

Pastor Taiwo Dina
Global Life & Power Assembly
Jos, Nigeria

Introduction

"I will praise thee for I am fearfully and wonderfully made. Marvellous are thy words: and my soul knoweth right well." (Psalm 139:14)

God is good, faithful and does not forsake those who trust Him. Throughout the Bible, we find that His methods of operation may change but He Himself remains the same.

No one can fully conceive or understand what God can do for those who believe and trust Him.

Who can measure, fathom and quantify His might? Who can accurately recognise or describe how big and great God's plans are towards those who love and trust Him?

O, for a thousand tongues to sing of my great Redeemer's praise, the glories of my God and King, and the triumphs of

His grace.

Life is a battlefield of which some battles start right early in life while others begin at a later time. At whatever stage the battles of life start, they have to be fought and interestingly, a Christian with an understanding of who he/she is in Christ, will surely overcome.

Troubles come against God's children but they are not meant to destroy us. Instead, some of them are meant to test our identity as children of God while some are to teach us about total reliance on God. When we overcome in these trials, then God is glorified.

"Now thanks be to God, which always causeth us to triumph in Christ, and maketh manifest the savour of His knowledge by us in every place" (2 Corinthians 2:14)

Our life in Christ is a glorious one. This does not mean that we will never be attacked or face adversity but the plan of God for us is that we triumph. What we do during an attack or adversity will determine whether we end up victorious or otherwise, even though our victories are guaranteed in Christ

I have gone through a lot of troubles in life but with God by my side, I am still standing. I have been down times without number; but I am still standing in the game. Do you know why? My heavenly Father holds the whistle and He determines the winner of the fight. Many of His children would have quit in defeat but His mercy saw us through and gave us victory.

God wants to answer many of your questions. He wants you to have a clear understanding of the truth concerning the reason certain things happen the way they do, so that you can still trust Him even when you cannot trace Him.

In the Bible, we find wonderful and powerful stories that establish the fact that God can actually allow His people to pass through certain unpleasant and impossible situations before they experience a breakthrough and victory. God is sovereign: He can deliver either from adversity or through it.

No wonder, Apostle Paul declares in 2 Corinthians 4:8-9 that "We are troubled on every side, yet not distressed; we are perplexed, but not in despair".

A lot of things came against the Israelite's glorious destiny; to stop them from getting to the Promised Land. Just as the enemy attacked them then, so does he attack God's people now.

Our Lord Jesus was not spared from the attack of the

enemy in the days of His earthly sojourn. The devil attempted to kill Him before He got to the Cross of Calvary, but like I said, when God is involved in a matter, He does not blow the whistle when His children are down. The God whom we serve is the One who changes times and seasons. Yes, He is the Game Changer. When He opens a door, no one can close it and when He closes a door, no one can open it. He is the Righteous Judge who steps into the case of His children at the right and appointed time. He never comes late and does not operate by season and time as we do because a thousand years are just like a day in His sight.

Many times when we go through trials and troubles, we tend to forget all the promises of God concerning us. I want you to remember that "God is not a man that He should lie; neither the son of man that He should repent: hath He said, and shall He not do it? Or hath He spoken, and shall He not make it good?" (Numbers 23:19).

People do fail, break promises and commitment; but not so with God. When He says, He does what He said. God's promises are firm. He never fails (Psalm 89:24, 33-34).

Do not listen to and do not believe the lies of the devil

when he comes attacking your mind and thoughts seeking to plant the seed of doubts, worry and fear.

You can count on the promises of God. He said that he will not leave you until He has done for you that which He has promised you (Genesis 28:15).

Over the ages, God's absolute trustworthiness has been demonstrated consistently. God fulfilled every promise He made to Israel and not one of them failed. "… not one of all the good promises the Lord your God gave you has failed. Every promise has been fulfilled; not one has failed" (Joshua 23:14 NIV).

God is still on the throne. Do you think that your case is more impossible than that of the Red sea? (Exodus 14:16-30). Or, perhaps you have not heard about the virgin who got pregnant, without sexual intimacy but through the power of the Holy Spirit? (Luke 1: 35) Mary said unto the angel that brought her the message from the Lord, "how shall this be...?" He Who created you knows "how" even though your situation may seem impossible just like it was with Mary. Just believe! Mary did just that.

There may seem to be no way for you just as it was with the Israelites. Do you know why? You are human. If things seem impossible with you, they are not so with God, "for with God nothing shall be impossible" (Luke 1:37)

When impossibility comes face to face with the power of God, the impossibility must bow. Don't give up your hope; instead, pick up your faith as you go through this book because at the end of the tunnel, light will shine. Halleluyah!

1

My Background

I am Pastor (Mrs) Charity O. Dina. I hail from Edo State. My husband, Pastor Taiwo O. Dina and I pastor the Global Life and Power Assembly in the city of Jos, Nigeria; and we are blessed with three grown up children - a daughter and two sons.

I was born, in Jos, into a Muslim family of Alhaji Ali Giwa who was a devout Muslim. We were raised up in a Muslim way of life: being strictly under control and supervision like the women in *purdah*. My father was a polygamist and had wives who were from tribes other than his and my mother's tribe. He had wives from the Hausa and Fulani tribes and they all practiced Islam with their children.

As a disciplinarian, my father did not allow us to go out of the house for any purpose other than to be driven to and from school by any of his drivers. Remaining indoors most of the day was the norm. In those days, whenever we peeped outside, we were always conscious and apprehensive of our father's return. Just hearing the sound or the hooting of his car horn was enough to send the shivers through our bodies and make us scamper back into the house. Till today, I am still affected by that way of life and as a result, I find it difficult to readily go out of our house or stay out late.

I thank the Lord for my background; it is not all negative and disadvantageous. My not being exposed to many vices, helped me to have a sense of contentment even after embracing the light of God's salvation through Jesus Christ.

Growing up in a Muslim home was funny, because we always dressed up in two wrappers and people will address and show us respect as though we were married women. This also affected my dress sense, because I now dress with outmost decency.

2

Coming to Jesus

"Neither is there salvation in any other: for there is none other name under heaven given among men, whereby we must be saved." (Act 4:12)

"Jesus answered and said unto them, verily, verily, I say unto thee, except a man be born again, he cannot see the kingdom of God." (John 3:3)

"And they said, believe on the Lord Jesus Christ, and thou shalt be saved, and thy house." (Act 16:31)

My mother, Mrs. Grace Giwa, was the first wife of my father. While she was with him, she maintained and practiced her Christian faith. She was the only Christian in the house and was a member of the

Evangelical Church Winning All, ECWA (formerly known as Evangelical Church of West Africa). She got separated from my father eventually, because of several issues, particularly, her refusal to convert to Islam.

When she got separated from my father and moved out of the house, she did not totally severe her contact with us, her children. In fact, she kept arranging for some Christians from the ECWA denomination to come to our house and preach the gospel of Christ to us, whenever our father was away. Initially, we did not embrace the gospel, probably because of the environment we were in or because the time was not ripe.

Eventually, in the late 1970s, a Gospel Crusade was scheduled to hold at the open field located opposite the then palace of the Jos Chief (Gbong Gwom Jos). We saw an advertisement of the event in a newspaper and for some strange reasons, we (my older sister and I) made up our minds to attend the programme. When the time came, we came up with a plan that would give us a good excuse for going out of the house: we claimed that we were sent on an errand and because none of our house-helps knew the location, we were to deliver the missive ourselves. That was the tale we asked my father's wives to tell him when he returns home and asks of our whereabouts.

But seek ye first the Kingdom of God, and His righteousness; and all these things shall be added unto you. (Matthew 6:33)

God is our refuge and strength, a very present help in trouble. (Psalm 46:1)

While growing up as a teenager, I normally had a rough time during my monthly menstrual period. The pain was usually so terrible that I often rolled on the floor in agony. I remember my mother taking me to a native doctor in search for a solution to the monthly horror. The native-doctor asked that we bring a live chicken as well as a couple of other items, so that he will put together a cure for the problem to which my mother agreed. Just as we were about to leave the native doctor's presence, he looked at me sternly and said, "If you like, you can come back because I can see that you are not happy that you were brought here." He was correct, I never liked the idea of being taken to him (the native doctor) at all. My mother dutifully purchased all the items that were demanded by the native doctor, including the live chicken. However, as Destiny would have it, the Gospel Crusade began three days before the set date of the appointment with the native doctor.

My older sister and I went for the first day of the crusade and it was a wonderful experience. We heard preaching from the Bible in a way we had never heard it before. The message was centred on the salvation of souls. When an altar call was made, we did not hesitate to step out of the crowd to join those who made the decision to surrender their hearts to the Saviour, Jesus Christ.

After this, another altar call was made for the purpose of praying for those who were sick. I was part of those who responded to the call. Hands were laid on me and prayer of healing and deliverance was offered.

"I am the Lord that healeth thee." (Exodus 15:26)

"Who forgiveth all thine iniquities; who healeth all thy diseases" (Psalm 103:3)

"He sent His word and healed them" (Psalm 107:20)

"Behold I am the Lord of all flesh: is there anything too hard for me?" (Jeremiah 32:27)

When my mother told me that we had to go back to see the native doctor, I refused flatly. She asked me what she was to do with the chicken and the various items she had bought. I told her that we should kill and eat up the chicken. That was exactly what we did.

To the glory and honour of the Lord Who does great things that are past finding out, my menstruation came the next month without any pain. God took away the pain and it has never returned till today and will never return because "...whatsoever God doeth, it shall be forever: nothing can be put to it, nor anything taken from it: and God doeth it, that men should fear before Him" (Ecclesiastes 3:14).

I believed that one of the reasons why God healed and delivered me from that affliction was to discourage me from ever putting my trust in any native doctor and to establish in me, a strong trust in the His own awesome power.

3

The Cost of Coming to Christ

"He that loveth father or mother more than me is not worthy of me: and he that loveth son or daughter more than me is not worthy of me. And he that taketh not his cross, and followeth after me, is not worthy of me. He that findeth his life shall lose it: and he that loseth his life for my sake shall find it." (Matthew 10:37-39)

If a person is not willing to give everything over to Christ, then he or she is not worthy of Him. We must be willing to give up everything to the Lord in total surrender because He gave up everything to purchase our salvation from sin and hell. We must be willing to give up our desires, dreams, and ambitions in order to embrace whatever may be God's will and plan for our lives.

After my sister and I became born again, we started sneaking out of the house to Bible teaching programmes and the zeal to serve the Lord began to increase rapidly in us. We became zealous about sharing the gospel with people; desiring that they too, would be saved like us. As a result of this passion, we joined the Personal Soul Winning Group of the Ministry that organised the Crusade in which we got saved. Sneaking out of the house to attend fellowship meetings and sneaking back into the house became the order of the day. We were secret disciples of the Lord Jesus and we were enjoying it until our cover was blown.

We returned home after attending a Bible study fellowship and learned that our Dad had returned home earlier than usual and was also sitting in the waiting room where he normally received his guests. To sneak into the house, we must pass through where he was seated. This situation filled us with great apprehension and dread. We knew that we were in trouble and must quickly find a way out of this tight corner. I suggested to my sister that we should pray that the Lord will temporarily make our Dad blind so that we can walk past him and into the house without being detected. Her response was, "how can that be?"

After a little while, I went aside to a corner near our house and bowed my head in prayer. I asked the Lord to grant that our Dad would not see me as I walked past him into the house.

To my amazement, God granted my request. My sister later walked into the house and was accosted by our Dad who angrily told her to go back to where she was coming from. Of course, she did not sleep in the house that night, it took the intervention and the pleading of several persons before our Dad re-admitted her into the house. By this time, it had become very obvious to most members of our polygamous family that we had stopped praying in the Islamic way and that we were instead reading the Bible, praying the way Christians do and were attending church services.

Our father was becoming more worried, dissatisfied and angry with the development. We knew he was looking for a good opportunity to catch us and express his disapproval concerning our strange behaviour. The opportunity came not too long after. As usual, my older sister and I went out on Evangelism in the company of some brethren who were passionate about winning lost souls to the Lord. I remember vividly, that on that particular day, the Lord helped us in leading several souls into making a commitment of their life to the Saviour. Our joy that day knew no bounds.

However, this joy was to become short-lived because an unexpected event happened that altered many things in our lives. While we were out on the streets that day doing Personal Evangelism, we did not know that our Dad was trailing us. The moment came when he drove his vehicle and packed at a vantage point where he was able to make full eye contact with us. The look on his face was that of shock, anger and disappointment. That day, we knew that something must give way as we were caught red-handed by no one other than the man who had the power to disown us.

"But and if ye suffer for righteousness sake, happy are ye: and be not afraid of their terror, neither be troubled; But sanctify the Lord God in your hearts: and be ready always to give an answer to everyman that asketh you a reason of the hope that is in you with meekness and fear."
(1Peter 3:14-15 KJV)

When we got home that evening, our Dad summoned us into his parlour. He expressed his outrage at our new life style. As far as he was concerned, we were bringing shame to him and it was a taboo for his own children to be carrying the Bible and preaching on the streets. Our Dad asked us to choose between him and our Pastor. I remember boldly telling him that the issue was not one of choosing between him and our Pastor, rather, it was a matter of choosing between him and choosing Jesus. He did not hesitate in deciding the matter there and then. Our Dad instructed us to pack out of his house and that we should go and meet our Pastor to pay our school fees, and our Jesus to take care of us.

"Blessed are ye, when men shall revile you, and persecute you, and shall say all manner of evil against you falsely, for my sake. Rejoice and be exceeding glad: for great is your reward in heaven: for so persecuted they the prophets which were before you."
(Matthew 5:11-12 KJV)

Our Dad was a rich man. He had lots of money, properties and plots of land. But we had to pack out of his house that day and went in search of where to stay. After squatting with different people for some time, we succeeded in securing a rented apartment at Audi Lane, behind the State Fire Fighting Service Headquarters in Jos.

Our decision to believe in Jesus Christ and serve Him, cost us a lot. Our education was truncated; food to eat became scarce and clothes to wear became a struggle. All these were because there was no more regular financial provision for us. Our Dad never looked back on his decision to kick us out of his house and never reached out to us with anything whatsoever.

Life became a big struggle with many painful experiences and times of shedding tears but with no regret for the choice we had made. We were not bothered because the joy of salvation kept us going and we knew that our suffering was nothing to compare with the love of Christ for us and the price He paid to redeem our soul.

"And everyone that hath forsaken houses, or brethren, or sisters, or father, or mother, or wife, or children, or land, for my name's sake, shall receive an hundred fold, and shall inherit everlasting life." (Matthew 19:29 KJV)

As a result of my resolve to wholeheartedly follow the Lord, there were times my sisters felt that I was being overzealous but I didn't let their opinion affect me. I somehow knew that the Hand of the Lord is upon me and I could not but just set my heart on seeking to know Him more and more as well as despise anything that may be a hindrance to fully following Him. Giving up my prestige, my father's love and care, as well as the plans he had for us was not too much a price to pay in exchange for the love of Christ. It was just about the period that my Dad was making concluding arrangements to send my older sister and I to Mecca on pilgrimage that we got converted to Christianity. Many people felt we had been hypnotised or have lost our senses. But we knew that they were wrong and the decision that we had made was the best.

In fact, when our father died and we went to greet his wives and our step brothers and sisters, we met with several people who didn't know that we were his children until that time. They expressed their shock upon discovering that we were his children and were not Muslims. We were told about how good, generous and considerate he was to them. The many properties that our father left were sold by our step brothers and we were told point blank that we would not be given anything as inheritance because we were considered as infidels.

In those days, our zeal for the Lord and passion for winning souls was so strong that no one visited our home without hearing the gospel preached to them. This issue generated a lot of negative talk to the point that our family relations in our home town were told that it appears like we had gone mad and that our attitude was causing people to stay away from us. It is not that we were mad, it was because we had seen the Light after been delivered from spiritual blindness. Also, we had made the choice like Moses did in Egypt, "to suffer affliction with the people of God, than to enjoy pleasure of sin for a season" (Hebrew 11:25)

4

Called to Ministry

"Who hath saved us, and called us with an holy calling, not according to our works, but according to his own purpose and grace, which was given us in Christ Jesus before the world began" (2 Timothy1:9)

We continued to deepen our devotion to the Lord and serving Him in practical ways as much as time will permit and somehow, I started sensing the strong desire to serve the Lord in more serious and full time way. It started dawning on me that the Lord was calling me into the ministry of the gospel of our Lord and Saviour. Fear gripped my heart and the whole idea was a little bit confusing. I thought I was not qualified, not prepared and that I may be getting a little bit over zealous in my understanding of what it meant to serve the Lord. I decided to really give the idea some serious time of prayers and I also sought the counsel of some preachers of the gospel. A good number of them prayed with me and they indicated that they believed that there is a genuine call into the ministry upon my life and that I should go and receive training in a formal Bible School in order to be equipped with basic knowledge in Theology as well as acquiring practical ministry skills. After some time, I made up my mind that stepping into full time ministry was God's will and that I would also seek admission into a reputable Bible School for training.

This decision did not materialise immediately because I would later discover that God has some other aspects of His plans for my life to put in place

.

5

Marriage

"But if you do marry, you have not sinned; and if a virgin marries, she has not sinned. But those who marry will face many troubles in this life, and I want to spare you this." (1 Corinthians 7:28)

The subject of marriage was not uppermost in my thoughts for a long time after I became born again. In fact, I was even contemplating remaining unmarried and just serving the Lord as a single person. This was because I was entertaining the thought that marriage could be a hindrance to my zeal and passion for preaching the gospel as well as singing for the Lord.

Several Christian Brothers came around and

expressed their interest in my older sister and me. Some of these men came out of pity for us and offered to start paying our school fees and also help in providing food and finances. We vehemently turned down their advances because of the solid foundation we received through the teaching of the Word of God from the servants of God who disciple us.

My anti-marriage mindset continued to influence me until one of my uncles had a talk with me. I also took time to fast and pray about the issue. Eventually, my mind began to entertain the possibility of getting married to a Christian man that would not be against my dream of serving the Lord in very tangible ways.

I remember vividly that several men of God came around and at different times, expressed their interest in marrying me. It was only one of these men that persisted and patiently pursued his desire to marry me to a logical conclusion.

Pastor Taiwo Dina, the then Senior Pastor of the Jos Headquarters branch of The Church of God Mission International (Overcomers' Faith Centre), showed up in our house one fateful evening. We (my older sister and my immediate younger sister) wondered what his mission was. He kept visiting and was very tactical in his ways. He did not indicate which one amongst the three of us he was interested in, for several months.

However, the day came when he showed up in my office at the then National Union of Food, Beverages and Tobacco Employees, Jos. After that visit, I didn't need to be told by anyone that he had feelings for me and that he was waiting for an opportune time to come clean with his intention.

Eventually, Pastor Dina proposed to me, telling me strongly that he believes I'm supposed to be his life partner and that he wanted me to take time to pray about the matter. I asked him to give me time to reflect and pray over the issue. This was particularly necessary because more than three people had claimed that they were convinced about me being their wife.

I took time to pray about who amongst my suitors was the will of God. I started sensing that it was likely going to be Pastor Dina but I had a concern about his being a Pastor. I did not want to marry a Pastor because it would mean being confined, most of the time, to ministering within the four walls of a particular church. I was of the opinion that marrying an Evangelist would afford me the opportunity of travelling to different places in the course of preaching the gospel.

This issue gave me so much concern that I couldn't give Pastor Dina a clear and positive answer for a long time. I sought the counsel and prayers of some men of God, including Uncle Peter Ozodo whose input as well as that of his wife, Aunty Moyo, was very helpful in sifting through the several confusing concerns I had over the delicate issue of who to say "yes" to amongst the several men who wanted relationship with me, with the view of marrying me.

At a point, Pastor Dina made it known to me that it was as clear as daylight to him that we were meant for one another. Whenever he visited our home and met any of the other men who were seeking for my hand in marriage, he never showed any sign of being disturbed. He made it clear to me one day that whenever he comes and sees any of those men, he would say in his mind, "You are wasting your time because the Lord has spoken that she is mine".

Eventually, I became convinced that the Lord was showing me that it was His will for me to marry Pastor Taiwo Dina. So I said "yes" to him and we started courting. As the plans for solidifying our relationship into marriage kicked off, we encountered some resistance from some of my relatives in my hometown. When they got to know that the man I wanted to marry is Yoruba by tribe, they raised objections.

Their reason for opposing my choice was traceable to the bitter experience our extended family had with the widow of my late journalist uncle, Mr. Dele Giwa. Being a Yoruba woman, the rough experiences that our family had with Funmi Giwa made them become biased against any Yoruba person marrying one of their own.

By the grace of God, we overcame all the challenges that confronted us and we got married on Saturday, 24th October, 1987.

The founder of the Church of God Mission International, late Archbishop Benson A. Idahosa was billed to officiate the wedding but due to some development that required his presence, he travelled out of the country and so could not be in Jos for the wedding. But his immediate deputy, Bishop J.B.S Coker, as well as several other Senior Ministers from within and outside the city of Jos graced our wedding ceremony. It was a well-attended, glorious wedding service and I am still able to recall vividly, the different events of that day as well as the people who graced the occasion from far and near.

Recalling the various developments that finally resulted into holding the wedding on 24th October, 1987, rekindles in me the fire of trust in God's faithfulness, goodness and mercy. God is truly awesome, dependable and worthy of our praise, worship and service.

6

How Marrying My Husband Has Helped Me

Marrying a man of God was a privilege. It has given me the opportunity to serve God without any hindrance. But it has been a privilege that came with so much responsibility.

To some ladies, marrying a man of God, particularly a Pastor, affords them the opportunity to live a glamorous life of being addressed as "Mummy" as well as dressing up flamboyantly. But you see, marrying a minister of the gospel is much more than such mundane reasons. If you really want to please God, it would not be cheap and worldly considerations would mean little to you because God brought you into the life of that servant of God to fulfil a divine purpose.

There was this day in which the Lord ministered to my heart that whenever I have the opportunity to minister to women, I should tell them that they didn't come into this world just for the purpose of marrying and procreating. No, every woman has been ordained to fulfil a divine purpose (destiny).

Married women must recognise that they have to bring in balance into their life and that as saying goes, "charity begins at home". God and His Word must be reflected in whatever we do, and whatever we do outside should be an extension of what we do at home.

Marrying my husband has really been a blessing to me. I used to be a very, very shy and reclusive person, but by God's grace and the encouragement my husband gave me, I was able to come "out of my shell."

7

Trials, Challenges, and God's Deliverances

"Many are the afflictions of the righteous: but the Lord delivereth him out of them all". (Psalm 34:19)

"My brethren, count it all joy when ye fall into divers temptation; knowing this, that the trying of your faith worketh patience" (James 1:2-3)

"Yea, and all that will live godly in Christ Jesus shall suffer persecution." (2 Timothy 3:12)

The Bible teaches us that trials and troubles are part of the package we received when we got saved and became followers of Christ. Although, going through trials, challenges, and troubles is normally not a pleasant experience, all Christians and non-Christians must have their own share.

After settling down as a newly-married person, my own share of trials began in the area of pregnancy and childbirth. The very first pregnancy I was blessed with, was carried for only a couple of months before I experienced a miscarriage. I remember clearly that I went into the toilet to ease myself, at least so I thought. But it turned to be a different and nasty experience. After I finished easing myself, I noticed that I was still dripping and it was bloody, too. At the end of this shocking event, I lost the pregnancy. It was a big blow to me, I had never previously been pregnant and was at a loss as to what was happening. With the encouragement and prayers of my husband, I took the matter in good strides and looked forward to the Lord proving Himself faithful to us.

A couple of months later, it was confirmed that I was pregnant, again. I was elated at the news and started looking forward to some problem-free months of carrying the pregnancy and eventually a time of quick, smooth and pain-free labour and delivery of the baby. However, this was not to be so.

When the pregnancy turned five months, I went for a

monthly ante-natal appointment at the hospital, like I had done the previous months. I was examined by the Nurses and the Doctor on duty that day at the ECWA Evangel Hospital (*Jankwano*), Jos. I was not expecting any negative findings from the various examinations that were carried out on me and the pregnancy, but I noticed that the Doctor's body language and facial expressions suggested that something unpleasant had been discovered. I asked what the problem was, but Dr. Omodele Oshunkiyesi, who was my Doctor and a member of our Church family, was not forthcoming with a definitive answer. I noticed the worried looks on her face. She requested to talk with my husband who had accompanied me to the Hospital. They both went aside and had a chat.

When they finished their side-talk, I asked Dr. Oshunkiyesi again, what the matter was, the response she gave me was "I don't understand what is going on" and that further tests needed to be carried out.

My husband, who was not satisfied with what he was told by Dr. Oshunkiyesi, requested that another person should examine me all over again. A senior resident doctor in the hospital and an expatriate, Dr. Trotsky was on duty that day. She was called upon to look into the matter and she proceeded immediately to carry out an examination on me. The outcome of the second medical examination was also not made known to me that day. My husband saw to it that the result of both Dr. Oshunkiyesi and Dr. Trotsky's findings were not immediately made known to me. He told me that the doctors detected some problems with the growth of the baby and that we should see to it that I took more rest. It will be much, much later that I would be brought into the knowledge of the truth of all that transpired on that day as well as that of the subsequent days.

My husband summoned several members of our church to our house and they spent a couple of days praying while I laid down flat on the floor. They were given instructions to pray mainly in tongues and to pray cancelling the agenda of hell against me and the pregnancy. I remember that those who participated in the prayer program included, Pastor Blessing Nya, Joseph and Samuel Odaudu, Toyin Ajepe, and some others I cannot recall now.

This prayer session of real spiritual warfare went on for 3 days after which we returned to the hospital and when another round of tests and check-ups was done, the doctor with excitement and a smile on her face asked my husband, "what happened?" and the answer he gave her was "a miracle happened." The baby in the womb that was previously pronounced dead is now back to life. It was at this point that I got to know that Dr. Trotsky and Dr. Oshunkiyesi had previously told my husband that we had lost the baby.

My husband, being a man of "stubborn faith", rejected their verdict and told them that he would want them to repeat their test the following day. They grudgingly agreed to this arrangement and the rest is history as it ended in victory because God over ruled and the baby came back to life and I carried the pregnancy for the full 9 months up till the day I started experiencing labour pains.

When the due date came around for the pregnancy to be delivered, I went into a prolonged labour that lasted for almost three days. The cervix kept dilating but slowly and I was in excruciating pain. We were all the while praying and trusting that the baby would be delivered naturally but this was not to be as the devil was determined to bring about his evil plans against me and my baby. I am convinced today that the forces of darkness, demonic and human were determined to kill my baby and I during the process of the child birth, but God had a better plan for us and for the glory of His Name.

On the third day of being in labour with serious pain

and agony, we prayerfully agreed that delivering the baby through Caesarean Section was a wise option. In fact, Dr. Oshunkiyesi had been putting pressure on us after advising that she was not supposed to allow me to continue beyond the point I had reached. My husband and I came to the agreement that an emergency surgery be carried out for the delivery. He signed the necessary papers and I was immediately prepared to be wheeled from the labour room to the Surgery Theatre which was some metres away.

God can save and does save His people from pain, suffering and evil. In His sovereignty though, He saves us through whatever comes upon or against us. He allowed me to go through some stuff but nonetheless, He demonstrated His Might and Mercy.

Shortly after I was being wheeled out on a stretcher to the theatre, I heard one of the Prayer Warriors from our church, Brother Fidelis (now Bishop Fidelis Ugbong of the Elohim Church) shouting at the top of his voice, saying, "There is cat following them, there is cat following them..." It turned out that a black cat was actually following us behind as the nurses were transporting me towards the operating theatre. My husband immediately gave instructions that Brother Fidelis and some of the brethren who were present that fateful morning should pursue the evil cat and kill it. I do not know if they succeeded in killing the cat but they chased it away and it couldn't follow us into the theatre.

Upon getting into the surgery theatre, Dr. Oshunkiyesi said to me, "Please ma, I would not be able to operate on you." I asked her what the problem was and she answered, "...you are like my biological sister and I don't know how I will feel when I cut you open." I responded to her with another question, "Oh, so you want to leave me in the hands of an unbeliever who doesn't hear God and may not know what to do or what not to do in the prevailing circumstances?" I told her emphatically that she is going to do it and that she should go ahead.

Dr. Omodele Oshunkiyesi stepped aside to go and pray to God. When she was done, she got back and said she was ready to carry out the surgery. In a moment, I could tell that I was becoming drowsy and sleepy and then I lost consciousness. When I finally came back to consciousness, I was greeted with smiling faces of several individuals and then I realised that my baby was there lying beside me. The Lord demonstrated His mercy, might and faithfulness by granting us a big Victory over the kingdom of darkness and its human agents.

"By this I know that thou favourest me, because mine enemy doth not triumph over me" (Psalm 41:11).

Dr. Oshunkiyesi gave us an account of what transpired in the course of carrying out the Caesarean section. She said that after cutting me open, her attempt to extract the baby was difficult. It was as though some invisible hands were struggling with her and pulling back the baby and that she could see me turning pale because I was bleeding heavily in spite of the measures she had taken to prevent much loss of blood. According to Dr. Oshunkiyesi, because of the prevailing circumstances, she quickly arranged for a blood transfusion to be carried out. The available blood in the hospital's blood bank was secured and I was promptly transfused with it. In those days, blood screening was a luxury and certainly, it was not carried out because more than twenty years later, it was discovered that I had an infection of Hepatitis C.

Another phase of trials, suffering and adversity started because I started falling ill back and forth and we could not put our fingers on the root cause of my frequent illnesses. There were times when I would become so weak in my body that I would literally have to crawl from the bed to any part of the house that I needed to go to.

I would never forget the experiences of a fateful day in which I was so sickly and weak that I thought I may die. My husband stood in the gap praying for me and anointed me with oil and claimed the promise of the Word of God from James 5:13-16 and Isaiah 54:17. He prayed earnestly for me and at a point carried me into our car and started driving around the city while praying fervently in both tongues and in the English language. We returned back to the house and I was able to walk out of the car, unaided and my health was restored.

For a very long time after this battle was won, I enjoyed good health and felt very strong in my body. However, I would still be confronted with "a new devil at the new level" the Lord was taking me to.

8

Other Childbirth Battles Fought and Won

The year was 1991 and the city was the biggest commercial nerve centre in the northern Nigeria, Kano. My husband had been transferred from heading the Church of God Mission International Incorporated, Headquarter Church in Jos, being the National Presbyter of the Plateau Province, to take up the leadership of the Kano Province.

I had never been to Kano and so, moving there opened me up to a lot of new experiences. The weather was very hot and the environment was dry and dusty, it was the opposite condition of the cool, calm "civil servant city" of Jos where I was born and had lived most of my life. Shortly after we arrived and settled down in Kano, a medical test confirmed that I was pregnant. I remembered very clearly that most of the nine months during the pregnancy, I was healthy and did not encounter any significant health challenges that normally accompanied pregnancy.

However, when the day of delivery came, I noticed that I had started bleeding and there was need for urgent intervention by a doctor. Contact was made with a Medical Doctor who owns and runs his own hospital. He examined me and immediately I was put on admission and was told that the baby was going to arrive by the evening of the same day. By noon time, when things were getting out of hand and I was still bleeding, my husband insisted that the junior Doctor on duty should call his boss to come and attend to the matter on ground. The young man returned looking gloomy with the report that his boss, the senior Doctor and proprietor of the private hospital was nowhere to be found in the hospital premises.

Much later, news came that the doctor, who we were banking on to take charge of the case, was found at his residence in a very drunken state, unfit to take care of himself, much less, administering any medical care on me.

Things kept degenerating as I was bleeding and also dripping water. Arrangement was made by my husband and some church leaders who had contacted another private hospital. I was immediately moved to Alasa Hospital and Maternity. As soon as the doctor and owner of the hospital, Dr. Alasa Abu, saw me, he instructed that I should be wheeled quickly into the Operating Theatre because it was surgery that will be required to save my life and that of my unborn baby. I noticed that Dr Alasa bowed his head and prayed before he started the procedure. This act of his, infused some courage and confidence in me that things will go well. You see, prayers can release the power of God to change situations and arrest the plans of the devil and his dark kingdom.

In Psalm 145:18-19, we read that, "The Lord is nigh unto all them that call upon Him, to all that call upon Him in truth. He will fulfil the desire of them that fear Him: He also will hear their cry, and will save them." The surgery went well and we were blessed with our second child, a boy. We named him Emmanuel, Oluwaseun, Oladimeji, Oghenahogie Dina.

The Lord proved Himself faithful in being with us and granting us victory in the battle that was fought. He indeed is the one who is almighty and does good to all. Before I was discharged from the hospital, we had a chat with Dr Alasa in his office. I remember him saying that we must go and "do thanksgiving to God" because of the great miracle of deliverance that He gave us. The doctor said that I had a ruptured uterus and that very few people normally survive the experience. Not only did I survive the trauma, my baby-boy was kept intact by the Lord's mercy.

Is it not amazing that the baby that the enemy was warring against is today a qualified and practicing Legal Practitioner? Our God is truly amazing and He has done us well and deserves our praise and adoration.

Although, the Lord over-ruled the devil's plans, I was no longer willing to have another child. I felt that since God has blessed us with two children, a girl and a boy, there was no need for a third child in view of the terrible experiences that surrounded the delivery of the two babies but God had a different plan for me.

Two years after the birth of Emmanuel in Kano, we had already relocated back to Jos. I found that I was pregnant, again! The emotion that came over me at that moment was a mixture of anger and fear. I was not willing to go through another crisis concerning child birth again.

However, much later, the Holy Spirit started

comforting me and infusing courage and faith in my heart. He helped me to come to the conclusion that God was aware of my situation and since he allowed it, He will take care of me.

When I began to attend ante-natal clinic and the Doctors at the hospital heard the story of the rupturing of my uterus, one of them advised to consider aborting the pregnancy because my life was at risk should there be another episode of a ruptured uterus. I told the doctor that "another ruptured uterus" was not my portion and that God is not wicked. In fact, we read in Proverb 10:22, that, *"the blessing of the Lord, it maketh rich, and he addeth no sorrow with it."* This scripture inspired faith in me to the effect that this third pregnancy was a blessing from the Lord to us and that no evil shall befall me nor add sorrow to this blessing of another child. Despite the negative opinions of the Medical Doctors and other persons concerning keeping the pregnancy, I choose to believe that God must have a glorious plan for the child in my womb. I did not ask for nor planned for the child and I was not going to terminate the pregnancy, I was willing to die for the child to live and fulfil destiny.

Of course, my husband was not in any way in support of terminating the pregnancy and so the matter was put to rest once and for all.

As days turned into weeks and weeks turned into months, I notice that my tummy was growing much bigger than usual at least in comparison to the way it did during the previous two pregnancies. At three months of the pregnancy, my tummy was so big that I could not easily bend over to the front. My tummy became very stiff around the area of my navel. I kept feeling as if my navel was being pulled and stretched. It was a strange feeling.

As the last trimester of the pregnancy approached, I started becoming more and more restless, my sleep was becoming more and more disrupted and all manners of discomforts began to set in.

At one of my regular ante-natal appointments with my Doctors, I was so overwhelmed with fear, pains, discomfort and other pregnancy related challenges that I demanded a Caesarean-Section be carried out for the delivery of the baby even though the pregnancy was not yet in the ninth month. The response of the doctor was an emphatic "NO"! With encouraging and sympathetic words, he talked me out of that idea. He told me that I had not come this far, to give up. I was inspired and strengthen to forge ahead with patience and faith until the due date of the delivery.

"...Fear not: for I have redeemed thee, I have called thee by thy name; thou art mine. When thou passest through the waters, I will be with thee; and through the rivers, they shall not overflow thee: when thou walkest through the fire, thou shalt not be burned; neither shall the flame kindle upon thee." (Isaiah 43:1-2).

When the expected day of delivery finally came, I sensed an unusual heaviness, worry and fear in my soul in a way I had never experienced before. I took time to pray and pour out my heart before the Lord. That day, I experienced the torment that the scripture refers to in 1 John 4:18 "There is no fear in love; but perfect love casteth out fear because fear hath torment. He that feareth is not made perfect in love".

After I was able to receive an impartation of faith from the Lord that day, I confidently went to the hospital to keep the appointment with the Doctor for the third and last Caesarean Section operation in this aspect of mother-hood. The surgery went quickly and smoothly without any negative development to the glory of the Lord.

However, the enemy did not fold his hands in attempting *"to steal, and to kill, and to destroy..."* (John 10:10). While I was still in the hospital recovering from the surgery I had under gone, my newborn baby-boy needed to be given some medication. The nurse on duty came into the room to administer the medication and this coincided with the presence of my friend, Rev. Dr. (Mrs) Nkechi Nwosu, who had come to greet me. Her visit on that day and at the time she was at my bed-side was ordained by the good and faithful Lord who always goes before His people to make the crooked path straight. As a result of Rev. Dr Mrs Nkechi Nwosu's keen observation, calamity was averted. You see, the nurse was about to administer an overdose of medication to my baby but she was stopped. There was no way I would have known what was happening because of my condition.

9

Health Challenges

"For I will restore health unto you and will heal your wound . . ." (Jeremiah 30:17)

For fifteen years after I trusted Christ with my life, I enjoyed good health. However, much later, when I started having some serious health challenges. One of the challenges started with my eyes. I experienced a lot of pressure in my eye such that when I look at people, they would think I'm deliberately dimming my eyes. The pressure came with a non-stop frontal headache that was so unbearable.

I visited the Jos University Teaching Hospital (JUTH) for a check and was told that I had *Glaucoma* -a disease of the optic nerve that could result in blindness. I was then introduced to an eye surgeon who told me to prepare for surgery. The prospect of a surgery did not scare me since I had my three children through caesarean section and God saw me through them all. However, I told the Doctor that I was unprepared for a surgery; so, he referred me to a hospital in Abuja, which had more sophisticated equipment, for proper testing.

At the said hospital in Abuja, they confirmed I had *glaucoma*. I decided to visit other hospitals and the results were still the same - *glaucoma*. In a particular hospital in Lagos, I was told that the condition could degenerate to blindness if not operated. Ironically though, the Doctor told me that the surgery was not a guaranteed success - that it could also fail. In fact, she told me that her own mother went blind as a result of the surgery. She introduced me to another doctor in Lagos University Teaching Hospital (LUTH). The doctor, Dr. Ari Baba, told me that he just finished operating someone with the same condition and that he could operate on me if I was ready.

"My peace I give unto you . . . let not your heart be troubled, neither let it be afraid" (John 14:27)

When I got home that day, I wept like a child and

prayed. I told God that I know He could save the situation with or without surgery. I prayed that He give me peace if He wanted me to do surgery because at the point, I didn't feel ready for a surgery.

I did not do the surgery in Lagos; so when I got back to Jos, the doctor I met in JUTH paid me a visit. I asked if he knew Eye Foundation because a Sister in church told me about the hospital during a discussion. The doctor confirmed knowing the hospital and even the second man in command, in the hospital. He gave me the man's phone number. I called the man and booked an appointment.

While we were praying and fasting about the condition, my daughter, Dr. Miracle Adejumo, had been praying and fasting for me, making declarations and plea that I would not go blind. She kept pressing me to go for another test.

It is good to teach our children to pray very early in life. We should continue to teach them until they own the Faith for themselves and are grounded in the Word. Children also imitate their parents and value what their parents' value. So, be careful what you model to your children.

"These words I command you today shall be on your heart, you shall teach them diligently to your children, and

shall talk of them when you sit in your house, and when you walk by the way. And when you lie down and when you rise." (Deuteronomy 6:6-7)

Teaching your children to pray, helps them to understand that God is always accessible and there for them. On the day of my appointment, I went to the Eye Foundation to see the doctor. A test was carried out and the doctor asked me: "who told you that you have *glaucoma*?" He went further to say that "Madam, even if you had *glaucoma*, it is just at the borderline and does not require surgery now". He wrote an intensive letter to the doctor in JUTH, demanding to know who told "this precious woman" that she had *glaucoma*. He told me to come back in six months' time for a check-up.

I did not go back till after a year. He checked my eyes and said, "Madam, you are okay, go and come back in a year's time". I did not go back till after two years because I had peace. He checked me again and told me to go and rest, "your eyes are even better than those younger than you". That was how God delivered me from *glaucoma* till today.

"And the Lord will deliver me from every evil work and preserve me for his heavenly Kingdom. To Him be glory forever and ever." (2 Timothy 4:18)

The enemy did not give up his attack on my health. I kept having malaria and typhoid - on and off. Everybody around me was worried and I kept praying about it while receiving treatment. One day, as I just ended a fast pertaining my health, my friend - a Pastor's wife, visited me. She told me that she just finished a fast regarding my health, and came by so we could both pray about it. I told her that she was in the spirit as I just finished a fast too and we prayed together.

That notwithstanding, the problem persisted for many years. If you see me healthy today, the next day when you see me again, you will think I've been sick for many months. It continued like that for many years till one day, another Pastor's wife came to see me in the office. She asked me why I was looking so pale and I told her about the persistent malaria and typhoid I've been battling. She asked if I've ever taken a *hepatitis* test because persistent malaria and typhoid are strong indicators of it. I told her "No"; so, I went for the test.

The test revealed I had *Hepatitis C*. At that time, I was supposed to go for a corrective surgery because of an error that occurred during one of my childbirths. After the *Hepatitis* was confirmed, I was asked to go for further tests which were very expensive. I had to do a Liver Function Test, before the surgery would be undertaken. After all the tests, I was ready for the surgery but it wouldn't go on because I had one last test to still take due to a new discovery from the results of a previous test. The tests result took over three months to be available and when it came, it was confirmed that I contracted the *Hepatitis C* from the unscreened blood administered to me during my first delivery.

I was referred to JUTH, where I was placed on a 3-month treatment. The drug I was to take for 3 months will cost one million naira per month. When I met the doctor I was referred to, Prof. (Mrs) Edith Okeke, she told me that, "you mean you have chronic *Hepatitis C* for many years and you are still looking like this? Some would have been bed-ridden by now". It was a miracle.

At that time, I kept making confessions that no organ of my body will be destroyed no matter what happened. That very year, the cure for the disease was discovered and the cost of the medication was reduced. The Consultant kept encouraging me to take the drug but I kept delaying. God touched me and healed me from all those afflictions.

"Many are the afflictions of the righteous but the Lord

delivers him out of them all." (Psalm 34:19)

In John 16, we find Jesus speaking to His disciples of the event that will soon unfold. They needed to hear these words of encouragement more than ever because He knew the hour of darkness that was soon to come on them. He taught them about the power of prayer in his name. He told them not to be surprised at the tension they would feel in an unbelieving world.

I took the medicine and went back for a test which showed that I have been healed! God is awesome. Sometimes when we pray about a thing, God doesn't necessarily answer in the way we want or expect, but one thing is sure, He always answers us. When someone is sick and prays to God, God can heal the person supernaturally or lead the person to the right source of appropriate medical treatment. In my case, God did the latter and also provided supernaturally for the very expensive treatment I had to undergo, and He made the drugs work! (some people take some drugs and don't get cured). Hallelujah!

God is the only reason I am still here. Over the years He has performed countless miracles – more than I can recount or put down in this book. He is still faithful in present times, still doing wonders but I would like to pause here to encourage you. Whatever the situation is in your life right now, you can be sure that God is aware and He cares about it. He never lets down those who hold on to Him, so keep holding on, He would come and save you. It also helps a lot to remember the victories God has given you in times past. Hold on to faith knowing that He is able to deliver you again and again.

That problem you are facing right now will not swallow you because greater is He that is in you than he that is in the world. Through Jesus you are victorious, you cannot be defeated, you will win in the end. You will look back over the challenges you are battling with now and you will smile. You will have a mind blowing testimony that you can, and should use to encourage others just like I am encouraging you now.

Now is the time to cheer up, raise your head and lift your eyes up to your Helper. Change your words from negative to faith-filled words. Don't accept defeat. As long as you are alive there is hope for you in Jesus and you will make it.

About The Author

Pastor Mrs. Charity O. Dina is an ordained Minister of the Gospel and an anointed Gospel Music Minister with a strong passion for leading God's people into intimate worship of the Lord. She is a gifted Songwriter with 2 recorded gospel music albums to her credit in the market.

She serves as the Vice President of their church ministry, Global Life and Power Assembly, Jos, Nigeria.

Pastor Charity was used of God to found the Special Women In Ministry International (SWIMI) and serves as the ministry's President.

She regularly reaches out to families through the Overcoming Family Conferences. She also has a regular outreach to widows.

Pastor Charity and her husband, Pastor (Dr.) Taiwo O. Dina, are parents to three adult children and the grand parents of two grandchildren.

Testimonials

Pastor Charity, who I fondly call 'Mummy' has been a mentor and spiritual mother to me since 2002. She has been a confidant and teacher. I have been greatly blessed by her willingness to make time to encourage, pray for, counsel, and support me through various seasons of my life and ministry. She has stood by me through the good times and the bad. Her example (together with Pastor Taiwo) of strength, courage, and integrity has been what has inspired me to keep standing in the midst of challenges and persecution. She has taught me the Word, modeled it, and challenged me to live it.

Thank you Pastor Charity for being you!

Pastor Mrs. Nandir Williams

To the GLORY OF GOD, I am testifying to the fact that the life of the Pastor Mrs. Charity Dina has blessed me tremendously. First of all, I want to thank GOD for bringing me across the path of this woman .... I have known her for over 20 years now.

I love her for one thing, she is a lover and worshipper of GOD, she is a powerful minstrel .... one who touches the heart of the Father when she sings. Whenever she sings, you yourself will know you have touch GOD. Another thing l love about her is the fact that she prays; this woman prays her heart even when her body is weak.

THANK YOU MA FOR ALL YOU DO FOR THE KINGDOM. I am grateful to GOD for your life Ma and pray that GOD will increase you the more with GRACE and WISDOM for the task ahead and STRENGTH to finish well in JESUS' MIGHTY NAME AMEN

Pastor Mrs. Kemi Love

My Encounter with Pastor Mrs. Charity Dina

The impact of God's Servant, Pastor Mrs. Charity Dina, on my life and Christian walk is immeasurable and dates back to over two and a half decades ago when I became a member of the Global Life and Power Assembly Jos Plateau State, Nigeria. From a distance and as a new member of the congregation I was awed by the fervency and power of her prayers, and her uncompromising stand on holiness and purity. Coming from a religious background where prayer and sin had a different definition and was lightly approached, I was challenged to unlearn my erstwhile religious disposition and begin a new life from the perspective of God's Word. My prayer life changed dramatically and my walk with God became more assured.

Over the years, I have had to work more closely with Pastor Charity in various capacities - as Men's Fellowship Leader, Head of some special Committees and the likes. I want to give God thanks for those opportunities because the Lord used them in birthing a new dimension in me as it relates to my current assignments. One remarkable occasion was when I was appointed to Chair the Planning Committee of the 2016 Special Women In Ministry Conference; a position I felt I was not prepared for. When I communicated my fears and unpreparedness to my Principal, Pastor Mrs. Charity Dina, I was taken aback by the words of strength and encouragement from a Biblical standpoint that I received. The patience with which she led me through how God uses imperfect people to accomplish His divine plan on earth left me with the thought that if she believed I could handle it, then I could. The Conference was held and though it was an international conference with its peculiar challenges, it was impactfully-successful to the glory of God. If God could pull it through for me on this, then I could trust Him all the way - even in bigger assignments.

Working with God's Servant has awaken faith in me and bolstered my understanding that it is God that works in me to accomplish His assignments through me. This has increased my dependency and confidence in Him. Today I sit as head of multinational delegations in my business and as a family and community head; and I can only give God thanks for the positive influence of God's Servant that has enabled me to honour our God in all my outings.

It is very difficult not to notice Pastor Charity's love and commitment to family, and understanding of hierarchy. In spite of the demands of her office and other ministry engagements she is able to ensure a visible quality family life. This one also got to me in a very special way. When a proposal is brought for which she could ordinarily take a position, it is common to hear her say she would need to clear it with her husband - our Senior Pastor. My wife and I have on many occasions had to draw inference from her disposition and this has been a stabilizing factor in our home.

Her personal character trait is contagious. It is difficult to be around her and not straighten up. For her, right is right and wrong is wrong. There is no sitting on the fence. Irrespective of what anybody thinks, truth must be said. She demands that as a child of God, you should be bold to speak the truth no matter the circumstance. In her relationship with all she has been unassuming and humble. This principle I have adopted, and it has helped to engender trust and confidence within my circle. Her caring and motherly disposition is worthy of commendation. She has the phone numbers of the young people in the church. Her calls and personal interaction with these children have helped to pattern their lives the Kingdom way and give peace to parents; and help to ease their parenting work. Her life of philanthropy is exemplary. I testify that I am a beneficiary of the grace, anointing, ministry, and Christ's life upon God's servant, Pastor Mrs. Charity Dina; and whole heartedly thank the Lord for the awesome privilege to be so blessed.

Mfon Essien

Praise be to God Almighty

Personally knowing Pastor Mrs. Charity Dina for almost 15 years and counting has been one of the impactful times of my existence. She has shown me and proven to be a true woman of God without compromise.

She has impacted me with her strong mind; not to be intimidated and to stand firm in my faith. She has groomed and trained me to be steadfast in the Word of God.

She has encouraged and helped me and my family in our downtimes; making sure we pulled through. Her conduct and way of life has been exemplary for me; in how I dress, communicate and relate with people. She also taught me to be bold and to tell the truth at all cost.

I admire every part of her ministrations. May God continue to strengthen you Ma!

Mrs. Gift Charles Kalu

A Life Transforming Experience

I came in contact with Pastor Mrs. Charity Dina and joined Special Women in Ministry International (SWIMI) then known as WIMI (Women In Ministry International) when a friend invited me to the Conference in 2005. Before this time, I had been seeing her from a distance especially during Life and Power Choir/Musical festival where Church Choirs in Jos were invited to Minister and I was usually with my Church Choir then to honor the program. I wasn't even married then. I remember vividly how Mama Dina, in her soft voice, will minister with so much of God's Power. Even as I write now, I could see those images of her popping up in my mind. Honestly, it has always been awesome sitting under Mama Charity's Ministry.

An outstanding testimony for me is the Spiritual growth. Apostle Paul said in 1 Corinthians 13:11 that *"when I was a child, I spake as a child, I understood as a child, I thought as a child: but when I became a man, I put away childish things."* This passage explains my story. Of course I was born again; but full of this *yayaya* lifestyle around the whole place. No discipline, flat character, and fleshly. However, sitting under Mama Charity's Ministry year after year, I always want to reflect the image of Christ. Flesh was constantly dealt with, for no flesh will glory in the Presence of God. Mama will always emphasize that we are not in a show, not for entertainment, it is Kingdom business. In a nutshell, reverence for God is paramount. I heard this consistently until Christ was formed. (and still forming) in me. Glory!

I dare to say that I have been built up spiritually. I have been taught, impacted, nurtured, and equipped through being exposed to anointed teachings during SWIMI Conferences.

A spiritual impartation I received by my association with Mama Dina is Prayer ... standing firm in the place of prayers. I can testify that God changes things. My life has taken a new turn because of this. I have learnt through her ministry that you birth your desires in the place of prayer. I can't thank God enough for this.

I sincerely praise the Almighty God who made my path meet with Pastor Mrs. Dina's. I have become a woman who is totally dependent on God and God has never failed me... He has always showed up strong on my behalf. To Him alone be all the glory.

And to my Mama, thanks for all your labour of love. Thanks for your listening ears, loving heart and your prayers... I'm so glad you gave.

Mrs. Oluwanifemi Oteh

Pastor Mrs. Charity Dina or 'Mama', as she is popularly referred to, has been my spiritual mother for over 20 years now.

My relationship with her took a more intimate turn when I joined the church. I observed that she leads an exemplary life. Most of the things she values are spiritual things and things all about God (emphasis on righteous living and being a true symbol of what you profess). This has really helped me in life and my daily living.

Words such as impossible have no place in Mummy's dictionary. There are many things I had doubted and thought were not possible in the past, especially whenever we're preparing for a conference. Mummy on the other hand would say they were already made available and truly the conference would come to pass and end gloriously.

All these has really helped my faith to trust God completely in all areas of life.

Mummy is a very prayerful person. She's never tired of praying whether alone or with people. Seeing her always praying is a motivation to me.

She's not only interested about my spiritual life but every other area of life including my business, my health and children.

Indeed, her impact in my life cannot be quantified. Knowing Mummy has helped me develop the potentials I never knew were inherent within me.

She gave me responsibilities that make me run to the place of prayer in order to execute them properly; praying and fasting to meet up to the set standard.

I thank God for His grace over Pastor Charity Dina (our Mama) and how far He has helped her in life and ministry.

I pray she conquers more territories and also that she finishes strong.

Mrs. Tayo Olufemi

I met Pastor Mrs. Charity Dina about 29 years ago when I joined Global Life and Power Assembly. Though I was born again, I still needed to grow in the faith.

Gradually, I became close to Mummy, as I fondly call her because that is who she has been to me: A true mother, Friend, Counselor, Encourager, and Prayer partner.

Mummy taught me how to pray and fast; and I am standing in the faith today by the example she has shown.

Whenever I am faced with any challenge beyond me, she's always a call away and she never hesitates to speak words of grace to me that would lift my spirit.

She has been an amazing woman and mother to me and my family by extension. A philanthropist who has a heart for people and a passion to see that broken homes are healed and restored. She is such a gift to this generation and I am blessed to be associated with her.

If I was asked to nominate the 'Deborah' of our time, the first person on my list would be Mummy Charity Dina.

I can attribute my standing in the faith today to my encounter with Mummy Dina who has taught me many spiritual disciplines including Fasting, Praying, Faith and Spiritual warfare.

There are not enough words to perfectly describe Mummy Dina whose heart of gold and love for God is worth emulating. I have nothing but love for her.

Congratulations Mum on this great feat, it is just the beginning of greater things to come.

Mrs. Esther Rasheed Kareem

Pastor Mrs. Charity Dina is a spiritual person. A person who fears God and is totally committed to obeying and doing what God demands from her to do and this makes it easier for her to relate to everyone as long as you are willing to follow God. She is an easy-going person who doesn't make herself unapproachable.

She is a lovely person who is driven by God's love and she wants everyone around her liberated from all kinds of limitations of inferiority complex and self–rejection. She believes that every child of God has a destiny to fulfill; and so she gives those who are willing to do what God has asked them to do an opportunity to do so.

Her passion for a godly home is another thing that cannot be taken away from her.

Pastor Mrs. Charity Dina has been a blessing to the Body of Christ and to me. I pray that God will continue to keep her to see and enjoy the fruit of her labour in Jesus' Name. Amen.

Pastor Mrs. Nora Louis Dunu

I first met Pastor Mrs. Charity Dina, fondly called 'Mama' in 1998 and ever since, her life and ministry has been a blessing to me and my family.

Mama is a woman of God and a woman of prayer. Her capacity to stand firm in the place of prayer is a gift and grace that I desire and covet so much.

Coming in contact with Mama, one will not be able to resist her deep insight in the Word of God and her zeal and passion for the Kingdom of God. Her ministry has blessed me and my family greatly, her Motherly Love has greatly impacted my life.

Talking of discipline, correcting and encouragement, I have benefited greatly from her. Her ministry through Special Women In Ministry International (SWIMI) has greatly transformed my life. May the grace of God ever grow stronger in her life and ministry. Amen.

Thank you for answering the call of God upon your life. You have been a blessing.

Pastor Segun Love

Testimony To The Person of
Pastor (Mrs.) Charity O. Dina

My first encounter with her was on New Year's Eve of 2002, when I first entered the former Life and Power Church Auditorium on Tafawa Balewa Street, Jos, Nigeria, where she was ministering from the pulpit in front of the church. Prior to this time, I had limited church experience and almost no real experience of female ministers ministering - talk less of with such great assurance, boldness, thunder, power, confidence in preaching, prayers, deliverance and warfare, with no fear or regard for the devil and his demons. I was stunned, shocked, impressed and won over to believe that if she can do it then I can also do it. A connection was established that I could not explain nor understand, but can best describe as a higher dimension of what I had with my biological mother who had gone to be with the LORD years before this encounter. Since then I have had many more encounters – some not to my liking but mostly for my good and joy later.

As a Minister of the Gospel, I've been privileged to watch and observe her life at close quarters. She, with her husband, have taken me under their wings as a son and have been teaching, discipling and mentoring me - a broken, unforgiving, arrogant reject, full of pride and bitterness into who I am today – a difficult task not made easy due to my natural tendencies and dispositions, but on my way to becoming the best version of me that God has designed. When many gave up on me, even when I gave up on myself, they refuse to give up on me. When many rejected me, and I even rejected myself, they accepted me unconditionally. I was sometimes the cause of great pain, concern, distress and even tears, yet her love and concern for me have been unshakable. Entrusting me with responsibilities and encouragements to go ahead, even when I feel incapable and inadequate and feel others are better suited and qualified to handle such positions and responsibilities.

I have watched and observed her high level of sacrifice and commitment to see to it that others' joy, comfort and fulfillment in life is paramount. Her infectious burning and consuming desire to see people, especially women, discover their talents, gifts, purposes and God's call upon their lives and give it expression by serving God, His people and their generations can be testified to by the ministry she pioneered, Special Women In Ministry International (SWIMI) amongst others.

One of her strengths is in her great trust in the LORD God and His WORD demonstrated by her insistence on Word-based prayer, consistency in the place of prayer and reliance on the "God that answers prayers"; evidenced by her slogan" TAKE IT TO THE THRONE AND NOT TO THE PHONE."

I marvel at the convicting, passionate, love and tenacity of this woman of prayer who carries prayer burdens on different levels (individuals, couples, families, organisations and nations). A lover of God and His presence, who loves worshiping "THE LOVER OF HER SOUL" and desires greatly to please Him and be more like Him, as well as being a vessel that He can work through (ready, prepared and available for His use). She believes in and does love giving (materially, financially, spiritually, smiles, hugs, pats, encouraging words, corrections and in many other ways) as she continually teaches us by word and strongly by her actions: "YOU CAN GIVE WITHOUT LOVING BUT CANNOT LOVE WITHOUT GIVING. "

Pastor (Mrs.) Charity O. Dina, as a role model worthy of emulation even though not perfect, is a strict person whom can be relied on to tell you, without deception, flattery or pampering, the truth in love. Her rebuke can be sharp but her quick embrace is soothing to the sick, wounded, hurt or broken. The aura of peaceful tranquility that is always around her dispels fear or worry. Her sensitivity to the Holy Spirit and her swift ability to pick and discern things and act upon what she is sensing, coupled with her disarming smile make her easy to relate with and confide in, as witnessed to by the large number of people who troop to her for counseling, prayers assistance and help.

In conclusion, she is a regal, firm, tough, no-nonsense disciplinarian, disciplined, reserved, yet a caring, quiet, gentle, adorable and loving person who is worth emulating and praising. My family and I are proud and ever grateful to the LORD our God for causing our destinies to cross with and to be associated with this great gift. We have continuously benefited from her large open heart.

Samuel O. Omirinde

Resources

Below are some of the ministry resources by the author:

I Am Grateful – CD

An album of 8 tracks all written and composed by Pastor (Mrs) Charity Dina

God Is Great – CD

An album of 8 tracks all written and composed by Pastor (Mrs) Charity Dina

For enquiries and bookings, call:
Miracle   +234(0)8066045252
Kunle   +234(0)8033549518
Samson Ojo   +234(0)7032840540

Printed in Great Britain
by Amazon

36990842R00056